"HAPPY DAYS!"

OSPREY
PUBLISHING

"HAPPY DAYS!"

*A Humorous Narrative in Drawings of
the Progress of American Arms*

1917–1919

BY

CPT. ALBAN B. BUTLER, JR.

First Division Museum
at Cantigny

First published in Great Britain in 2011 by Osprey Publishing,
Midland House, West Way, Botley, Oxford, OX2 0PH, UK
44-02 23rd Street, Suite 219, Long Island City, NY 11101, USA
E-mail: info@ospreypublishing.com

A CIP catalogue record for this book is available from the British Library

ISBN: 978 1 84908 629 5

Typeset in Centaur MT
Jacket design by Brainchild Studios/NYC
Printed in China through Worldprint Ltd

11 12 13 14 15   10 9 8 7 6 5 4 3 2 1

Osprey Publishing is supporting the Woodland Trust, the UK's leading woodland conservation
charity, by funding the dedication of trees.

www.ospreypublishing.com

FIRST EDITION
Library of Congress Cataloging-in-Publication Data (tk)

Front cover: Alban B. Butler, Jr.

CONTENTS

EDITOR'S NOTE

SOME readers may find the depictions of African-American soldiers in this book to be offensive. The First Division Museum chose to include them because they are Butler's original work and because they reflect the racial stereotyping of his time. To excise them from the book would be to ignore racist perceptions of the day as well as African-American soldiers' participation in World War I. No African-American soldiers served with the First Division, as far as is known, because the AEF, like the U.S. Army, was segregated. The approximately 350,000 African-American soldiers who served with the AEF served mainly in labor and support units and in two all-black divisions, the 92nd and 93rd, officered by whites. Although Butler's cartoons do not do justice to their service, all of his figures—French and German soldiers, doughboys, and American officers—are cartoon exaggerations embellished for comedic effect. The First Division Museum believes it is important to present Butler's work, and all historical artifacts, authentically.

PREFACE

AS Charles P. Summerall, the commander of the First Division during its major battles, wrote in the original foreword, Alban B. Butler, Jr.'s *"Happy Days!": A Humorous Narrative in Drawings of the Progress of American Arms, 1917–1919* is "a priceless record" of that famous division. Ten years after World War I, the proud veterans in the Society of the First Division published this collection of cartoons with brief comments that portrayed experiences of the unit from the ocean voyage to France, through the war and its months in the Army of Occupation, until its return to the United States in autumn 1919.

ST. NAZAIRE
First Division troops leave their transport ship in the harbor of St. Nazaire, France, on June 28, 1917. Company K, 3rd Battalion, 28th Infantry Regiment was the first unit ashore.

The First Division, one of the most distinguished units in the Army, was hastily organized in May 1917 in order to show the flag as soon as possible after the United States entered World War I. Leading elements landed in France in late June and began training under French tutelage. It was the first American division to go to the front, and it made the first American regimental attack at Cantigny in May. It confirmed its reputation in mid-July 1918 when it played a significant role in the Battle of Soissons, which many historians consider the turning point of the war. It fought in the St. Mihiel Offensive and played a crucial role during the Meuse-Argonne Offensive. In late 1918, General John J. Pershing issued a General Order that expressed his admiration for this division: "The Commander-in-Chief has noted in this division a special pride of service and a high state of morale never broken by hardship nor battle." He compounded this praise in a comment he made in General Summerall's 1922 efficiency report:

THE FRONT LINE IN PICARDY
The assault at Cantigny by French tanks and First Division troops on May 28, 1918. Notice the rolling barrage of artillery on the horizon as support infantry moves forward behind the assault troops.

General John J. Pershing addressing officers of the First Division at Chaumont, France, on April 16, 1918, before they leave for the line. Major General Robert L. Bullard, commanding the First Division, is in his fur coat.

"the American First Division had no equal in the World War."

Of the four generals who commanded the division during the war, Summerall served longest with the First Division, first as commander of the First Field Artillery Brigade that supported the attack at Cantigny. He was the division commander at Soissons and St. Mihiel, as well as throughout its great effort driving the Germans out of the Argonne Forest. During the last month of the war, he commanded V Corps during the final phase of the Meuse-Argonne. A West Pointer, he was well known as an outstanding artilleryman and troop leader. As the Field Artillery instructor at West Point from 1905 to 1910, he made a strong impression on cadets, including George S. Patton, who considered him a mentor. When the United States went to war, he argued effectively for more artillery in the newly created infantry divisions. A dynamic officer whom Pershing lauded in a postwar efficiency report for his "superlative qualities of character and leadership," Summerall was not a headquarters general but one who went out every day to the front and talked with many subordinate commanders and soldiers. He wanted to make certain they had the stamina and spirit for the fight, and promptly relieved the commanders who did not.

His aide throughout the war was Alban Butler. A 1913 Yale graduate who was in the oil business in Oklahoma when the war began, Butler attended one of the Plattsburg training camps prior to the war and quickly became a lieutenant after he entered the Army in 1917. That fall, he joined the 42nd Division and became an aide to Summerall, who had just pinned on his first star as commander of that division's artillery brigade, before his transfer to the First Division. Butler remained with the general throughout the war and wrote him later: "We were together over two years and they will always be the prize years of my life."

Before he entered the Army, Butler had honed his skill as a cartoonist in his

VANGUARD OF THE AEF

On June 14, 1917, 1st Expeditionary Division Headquarters and the first contingent of troops sailed from New York and Hoboken. On June 27, 1917, the first U.S. troops arrived at St. Nazaire, France.

contributions to the *Yale Record*. When he crossed the Atlantic with the 42nd Division, he contributed regularly to the ship's daily mimeographed newsletter. In late December 1917, when he went with General Summerall to the First Division's Field Artillery Brigade, he began contributing cartoons to the brigade newspaper. These cartoons reached a greater audience as copies circulated in other units, including the nearby French divisions. During the period the First served in the Army of Occupation, Butler's cartoons appeared regularly in the weekly newspaper. In this book, he has several caricatures of officers well known to First Division troops: Pershing, Summerall, Robert L. Bullard, Frank Parker, John L. Hines, George B.

BLACK DOUGHBOYS

African-American soldiers of Company B, 803rd Pioneer Infantry Regiment, digging entrenchments between Cheppy and Varennes-en-Argonne, Meuse, France, in October 1918. Only a small percentage of black soldiers saw combat in World War I. Because of racist attitudes and segregation, most were relegated to noncombat roles.

Duncan, and George C. Marshall among them. Readers acquainted with photographs of these officers should easily recognize them in these pages. The officers and soldiers who make up the vast majority of figures in the cartoons, however, often are caricatured in the manner of the "funny papers" of that period. The few black soldiers depicted, as well as the Germans and some of the French, are more comic in appearance than the doughboys.

Soldiers liked Butler's cartoons when they first appeared, and their enthusiasm continued over the years, as indicated by the First Division veterans' organization's desire to publish this volume ten years after the war. In a letter to his sister from October 1918, Butler made it clear that he was a keen observer. He provided her with a detailed description of the Meuse-Argonne battle scene: the heavy traffic of men, horses, and trucks on the three crowded roads into the area through the field hospitals; artillery positions; the area that had been captured earlier in the attack with German corpses; a crashed plane with two charred bodies of American aviators; reserve combat units where soldiers in foxholes are smiling and joking; and, finally, the front where most men are out of sight.

MOVING INTO THE MEUSE-ARGONNE

The First Division entered the shelled village of Cheppy, Meuse, France, on October 1, 1918. In this picture, the rolling kitchen has stopped to cook a meal. A truck in Butler's cartoon has the pentagon of the V Corps, commanded by Major General Charles P. Summerall at the end of the war. Butler was still his aide de camp.

PAS DE GAZ

Second Lieutenant Warren A. Ransom, Battery D, 6th Field Artillery of the First Division, wearing a French M2 gas mask. Every soldier of the division would have carried this as a back-up gas mask. The M2 was made from a resin-impregnated cloth. Soldiers wearing it looked like they had a duckbill.

Most of Butler's cartoons are panoramas of the situations that were familiar to those men. What helped them endure the difficulties and dangers they experienced was their sense of humor, so they appreciated his humorous approach. When he dealt with combat, he got across the dangers of poison gas and high-explosive shelling, a patrol capturing prisoners, and other battle scenes. He often included German airplanes and, in one cartoon, French cavalry attacking with their lances, but he did so with a sense of humor and without the gruesome aspects.

Although there is humor in nearly all the cartoons in this collection, one that portrays both realism and Butler's humorous touch—as well as demonstrates what amused soldiers in 1918 and ten years later—is "The March on Sedan" (p. 96). This cartoon depicts a long march during the last days of the war. In the foreground, a soldier with an arm in a sling is walking to the rear past a large shell hole. The central focus is a file of soldiers, most with grim, determined expressions, taking long strides. Two of the men ask questions that soldiers have probably raised in similar situations throughout history: "When do we eat?" and "Where the H_____ are them objectives?" In the distance are shadows of horse-drawn artillery and more marching soldiers.

After the war, Butler returned to a position in the National Oil and Development Company, of which his father served as president, and prospered the rest of his life in this business. In 1919, he married, but the couple did not have children. In 1948, Butler died of a heart attack. His obituary in a local newspaper identified him only as "a prominent Tulsa, Okla. oilman." There was no mention of his service in World War I or his talent as a cartoonist. The First Division and other AEF veterans, as well as those of us interested in that division and the AEF, appreciate and remember him for his work in *"Happy Days!"*.

—Edward M. Coffman
Professor Emeritus
University of Wisconsin–Madison
Winter 2011

"HAPPY DAYS!"

THE COMBAT COMMANDERS
OF THE FIRST DIVISION A.E.F.

Generals Bullard, Summerall, and Parker

FOREWORD

BY

CHARLES PELOT SUMMERALL, D.S.C.

MAJOR GENERAL, U.S. ARMY

Who Commanded the First Division, A.E.F., July 1918 to October 1918

TEN YEARS AGO a place was carved in the world's history by almost superhuman effort and sublime resolution, sacrifice, and valor. For all who served, whether in the homeland or at the front, the passing years but enhance the richness and pleasure of recollections of their service and their comrades of the World War.

Historians and war correspondents who served intimately and shared the hardships of battle have recorded the story of glorious victory, heroism of individuals, sacrifice and trials of battle. Time alone will make more accurate the innumerable and immeasurable tales of the exploits of the American soldier.

The First Division, the vanguard of the A.E.F., with its exalted spirit, contributed most brilliantly, by its privileged share, in the achievements of the A.E.F. Its experiences, however, were not unlike those of all other commands.

With the serious business of war and the tragedies and hardships of campaign and battle there were mingled lighter thoughts and amusing incidents. A sense of humor is characteristic of the soldier and it serves to help him to bear cheerfully whatever lot may befall him. The man who can contribute to his spirit of fun, and therefore, to his morale, is invaluable to any command. Captain Alban B. Butler, Jr., A.D.C., was rarely gifted in his keen sense of humor and his artistic power of expressing it. Figuratively speaking, he

wielded his pen as mightily as his sword and his cartoons constitute a priceless record of the days of stress and battle ten years ago. Veterans and those who followed them in their great adventure will find in these sketches happy reminiscences and awakened memories of pleasurable experiences when the ills of which they may have complained have been forgotten.

Major General, Chief of Staff

INTRODUCTION

"HAPPY DAYS!"

THE Society of the First Division A. E. F. is immensely indebted to Captain Alban B. Butler, Jr., for presenting these drawings and sketches to the Society and allowing them to be collected for permanent preservation in this book. Refusing all thought of gain through personal publication, Captain Butler has enriched the Society with a priceless record of the war.

To understand and appreciate these cartoons fully it is necessary to recall the situation in France in the Spring of 1918 and the events which created the "trench newspaper" for which Butler drew the first of them.

The First Division landed at St. Nazaire in June 1917. Other troops followed until in the Spring of 1918 there were six American divisions in France. During this time they had seen the gradual decline of Allied morale. British and French offensives had failed, Italy had suffered a crushing defeat, Russia had disintegrated, and America had done nothing but

TOUL

occupy quiet sectors and endure the rigors of the memorable winter of 1917–1918.

The long expected German spring offensive came at the junction of the British and French armies in Picardy. Reserves were badly needed and soon the First Division was withdrawn from the Toul sector and sent across France. Its opportunity had come and it was sent in to relieve a sorely tried French division facing Montdidier.

This was a different kind of fighting,

Lt. T. (7th F.A.)—Good morning, General.
C.P.S.—Everywhere I go my orders are disobeyed!
Lt. T.—Yes Sir!

THE ENGINEERS

and one much more to the liking of American troops. Gone were the deep trenches, the acres of rusty barbed wire and the ease of quiet sectors. Shells shrieked overhead incessantly day and night. Gas smothered positions only to force the batteries into others. Telephone wires were run and cables buried, while in the wheatfields which had become no-man's-land, the infantry and engineers met the flower of the German army. Every night there were patrol encounters while the shallow trenches were being dug.

The French, still sceptical of American ability, eagerly watched the experiment. At the end of a month, as the Americans more than held their own, the final test was permitted. On May 28th the First Division attacked, captured and held against furious counter-attacks the village of Cantigny. The French, now convinced, rated the American troops with the best of the Allied divisions.

The First Division, with spirits high, awaited its next mission, for the Second Division was coming up to relieve it, but the Second Division was diverted towards Chateau Thierry and it soon became evident that the First Division was to remain at Cantigny. The French Division on its left was sent to the active front and the First Division had to extend itself over both sectors.

Once more the Division faced the deadly routine of holding a defensive sector. Commanding officers immediately took steps to maintain the high morale which had so recently brought recognition to American arms. General Summerall, then commanding the First Field Artillery Brigade, instructed his intelligence officer to issue a daily bulletin of news, humor, base-ball scores, happenings on other fronts, and all the latest rumors.

CANTIGNY

Captain Butler—whose talent for drawing was known only to those who remembered his cartoons when he was chairman of the *Yale Record*—was then aide-de-camp to General Summerall and undertook to draw a daily cartoon as a comic supplement.

Printed on sheets of typewriter paper from a gelatin pad, the *"First Field Artillery Brigade Observer"* began its career as a daily "trench newspaper," and copies were sent with the day's orders to every battery in the Division.

The success of the *Observer* was immediate, largely because of Butler's drawings. Always funny, absolutely true in every detail of materiel and equipment, sometimes a little cynical but never bitter, his cartoons caught the fancy of the rank and file. The battery bulletin board was constantly watched for the latest issue.

THE DAYLIGHT RAID

The fame of the *Observer* spread. When the artillery liaison officers with infantry units received the first edition, the infantry demanded daily copies for every company. It was not long before every unit in the division insisted upon its right to be on the distribution list. Higher staffs let it be known that they, too, needed copies and the French divisions on either side intimated that it was part of trench courtesy to exchange all information. The gelatin pad was worked to its limit, so great was the demand.

One day the *Observer* appeared with a full page cartoon of every type of French soldier under the title "FRAWGS". It was not long before a polite request from a neighboring French unit for additional copies

FIRST FIELD ARTILLERY BRIGADE OBSERVER

As Seen From Our O. P.

With Illustrations

June 20, 1918.

Yesterday evening five Boches were proceeding along National Highway 55, comfortably seated in a wagon. American Artillerymen did not like to see a chance like this slip, so dropped a shell nearby. The Boches not wishing to be encumbered by a wagon in their retreat, jumped out, and started across country. The next shell landed in the party, and when the smoke cleared there were no Boches seen.

Earlier in the afternoon, another wagon was fired on by American artillery and when last seen was two kilometers down the road picking up speed with every stride of the teams.

A prisoner was captured last night by a raiding party of the 23th Infantry who visited the Hunich Trench. The raid was greatly assisted by the 7th F.A. The raider dispersed a working party on the way over and came upon a machine gun nest full of Boches which was quickly silenced by a Stokes Mortar bomb. The prisoner who was captured was dragged out of a shell hole and brought back. He belonged to the 3rd M.G. Co. 272nd Reserve Regiment of the 82nd Reserve Division. The prisoner stated that the Artillery fire had killed two and wounded 12 during the last six days in which his company was in the first line. The C.O. of the Battalion in line had to be changed on account of artillery fire.

The Boche official report of June 20, 1918, states that between the Meuse and the Mosolle, their storm troops penetrated deeply into the American positions near Seicheproy and inflicted heavy losses on the Americans.

The Austrian official is drawn out, but merely claims that the greater part of the Piave front had fallen.

Rumor. The latest rumor is that the Division will be here for another six months. This rumor has pretty well stopped the rumor that we are going to parade in everybody's home town on July 4th.

Aviation. Lieutenant Wusthoff, Bocheland's 4 ranking ace was brought down three days ago, probably by an Englishman.
Sergeant Baylies, an American flying in a French squadron is reported to have been brought down in flames day before yesterday.

The Boches are reported to have in use a bomb of 1000 kilos. They are particularly adapted to destroying Churches and hospitals and are probably marked with a red cross.

It has been established that the "Terror of the Skies" who dropped bombs all over this Sector is an American who was flying a British plane. He was brought down with a broken arm by Archies. When cured he will be furnished with a guide and sent out again.

FACSIMILE OF FIRST COPY OF "OBSERVER"

THE SHAVETAIL'S DREAM
ILLUSTRATION ACCOMPANYING FIRST COPY OF "OBSERVER"

SOISSONS

brought grave consternation to the Division Staff. Explanations were carefully prepared when it was learned that our Allies considered them the finest caricatures of the French Army ever seen.

The incidents of the day formed the topics of many drawings. One afternoon in a sector where supposedly no one could stir in daylight, a patrol crept across to the German lines. Slowly they worked themselves along, seized a drowsy sentry and brought him back a prisoner. The next *Observer* showed not only the capture, but also the fancied consternation of the German relief. Oddly enough, this raid was so impossible to the Teuton mind that, after much thought, a long order was issued cautioning all units that the Americans were using lassos from their trenches.

Early in July, the *Observer* officially passed into history. The First Division was relieved and sent to more active work. Never was there the opportunity to revive it during the bitter fighting which ensued between then and the Armistice. But the appetite, once whetted, demanded more and Butler continued drawing. Each engagement

AT CHARLIE'S BAR

brought forth more odd circumstances which he sketched in message book, letters, and for those at the mess.

Meanwhile the First Division, in rest billets, was hastily put aboard a truck train and, after a long journey and a night's march, found itself with the Second American Division and the First Moroccan Division in the great surprise attack on Soissons, which turned the tide of the War. Casualties and promotions in this five-day battle brought changes in command but little rest for the troops. Back

ST. MIHIEL

once more to Lorraine the "Hommes 40— Chevaux 8" sped. A brief rest was given by taking over a very quiet sector and some of the lucky ones got a few days' leave, among them Butler. Fortunately for posterity, he recorded what he saw in Paris and at Biarritz.

Events moved still more rapidly. The elaborate preparations for St. Mihiel were chronicled,

FRAWGS
FROM ORIGINAL HECTOGRAPH

MEUSE-ARGONNE

as well as the unforeseen ease and completeness of the victory. Then came the Meuse-Argonne offensive, which was in reality three great battles. As aide to General Summerall, who commanded the First Division and then the Fifth Corps, Butler saw the action from an ever-widening viewpoint. Day and night with the tireless Summerall, he caught cross sections of American army life.

He saw divisions recently landed from training camps in the United States hurled into the thick of the forty-seven day battle; brigadiers with their staffs in nice new uniforms vainly arguing with a tired M. P. about a one-way road; ancient mess sergeants somehow getting the rolling kitchens along. He saw the final break through and watched his old outfit fight its way forward thirty-eight miles in thirty hours in the forced march on Sedan.

The Armistice and the march up to the Rhine maintained the high pitch to which one year's constant fighting had tuned the First Division. But, once the Bridgehead was established, life became unutterably dull by

SEDAN

contrast. Many things were tried to maintain the high morale and among them another paper. This time it was more pretentious and was published weekly under the name "Bridgehead Sentinel". Butler was urged to contribute drawings and willingly complied. Gathering together all his sketches and redrawing the cartoons from the Observer, he set to work. All the humor and irony of situations and personalities came forth once more in ninety large drawings.

The Bridgehead Sentinel was published regularly until the return home of the Division. Then once more it was started, but could not survive the reduction of personnel and the distribution of the Division units among different posts. During its existence it had managed to publish somewhat less than half of Butler's drawings.

Steadily the demand for publication has grown. Old copies of the Observer and the

THE CAPTURED COLONEL

Bridgehead Sentinel have become dim with use, while as yet half the drawings have lain in the Society's files unpublished in any form. Meanwhile, Butler has drawn for various occasions small sketches of familiar characters, incidents and illustrations of old songs, and has presented these also to the Society. The tenth anniversary of the Armistice has been chosen by the Society as the fitting time to publish all the military drawings of Captain Butler.

CHANGES IN COMMAND

Drawn originally to amuse the personnel of one field artillery brigade, these sketches are in no measure local. They cover every phase of a soldier's life in France and will bring back to all a flood of memories of the lighter side, the inevitably humorous side, of the war.

"HINKY-DINKY-PARLEZ-VOUS!"

The Drawings of
CPT. ALBAN B. BUTLER, JR.

VANGUARD OF THE A. E. F.

AT THE request of the Allies, the First Division was formed from existing units of the regular army and, on June 3rd, 1917, began the journey to Hoboken. All these units had seen much service in the Mexican disturbances and were in a high state of efficiency. They were filled to war strength by recruits and, upon arrival, were embarked secretly upon twelve ships. This first convoy, after four days at anchor in New York harbor, weighed anchor, and the troops cheered as they sailed on the great adventure.   *June 1917.*

"SHALL I LIVE TO FIGHT?"

ℭHE United States Navy took over interned vessels as well as all available American ships and sailed them throughout the war as transports. The imminent danger of attack by enemy submarines forced several innovations. Life preservers were worn by the soldiers at all times. After dark no lights were permitted, not even cigarettes; while all the day's garbage was collected in a huge bin on the forward deck and thrown overboard at midnight, so as to leave no trail. Preceded by a cruiser, the huge convoys zig-zagged apparently all over the ocean for twelve days. *June 1917.*

ST. NAZAIRE

On June 26th, the first American troops landed on French soil and went into camp outside St. Nazaire. The French soon welcomed their new and highly profitable guests, while the soldiers strove to master the language, briquets, vin-rouge, and the many interesting features of a foreign seaport town. *June 1917.*

"ENCORE!"

*I*T WAS often difficult to get the first drink, but luckily the French used some English words. "Encore," spoken in a loud voice would bring another bottle and more saucers with the price printed on them. The French, on the other hand, made one drink last all day.   *June 1917.*

SIDE DOOR PULLMANS

A BATTALION of the First Division was sent to Paris to march in the parade of July 4th, 1917. This was the first experience with French railroads. In contrast to American journeys, where army regulations provide for Pullman tourist sleepers, the American soldiers were introduced to the tiny freight cars. These sometimes carried forty soldiers and, at other times, eight horses. The remainder of the Division entrained soon after for the Gondrecourt and La Valdahon training areas.   *July 1917.*

LEARNING TRENCH WARFARE

THE 47th French Division of Chasseurs Alpins was stationed in the same area, and the First Division quickly learned not only the rudiments of trench warfare, but also much of the esprit of the "Blue Devils." Many of the weapons, such as grenades, trench-mortars, Chauchat automatic rifles, gas-masks and French 75's were new to American troops. Skinny French horses and even French mules had to be mastered, while British instructors taught the bayonet drill.   *August 1917.*

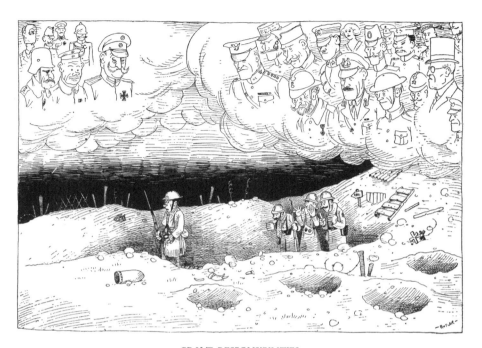

GRAVE RESPONSIBILITIES

𝒯ʜᴇ time had now come for the Americans to take their place in the battle lines. On the night of October 21st, 1917, units of the First Division occupied the front line trenches ten kilometers northeast of Nancy, and Battery C of the Sixth Field Artillery fired the first American shot on October 23rd, while, on October 27th, the first German prisoner was captured. The Germans, learning of the presence of American troops, broke the quiet of the sector with a raid. A sergeant and ten men were taken prisoners, and the first Americans were killed in action: Gresham, Enright and Hay.

October 1917.

HOTEL DU CHEVAL BLANC

*A*FTER a month of trench experience the Division returned
to the Gondrecourt training area, a dismal valley with
a town at each end. Ligny-en-Barrois, just outside the
American area, was the goal of everyone who could get a
pass. Many an infantryman learned much equitation on a
borrowed horse when, after retreat, he rode away for a
change from the inevitable "slumgullion" and "goldfish."
And here, too, he was introduced into fresh mysteries.
Saccharin bottles took the place of sugar and "tickets du
pain" were necessary. The food was always a surprise with
"cheval" or "escargots" as the foundation, but it was a change
and champagne was five francs a bottle.   *November 1917.*

THE MEMORABLE WINTER OF 1917–1918

GENERAL SUMMERALL, the Artillery Brigade Commander, stalled in a snowdrift, being rescued by one of his Aides.
December 1917.

PARLOR, BEDROOM AND BATH

"Chateau de Beaupré, First Field Artillery Brigade Headquarters near Gondrecourt, erected in the twelfth century,
the coldest place I was ever in."—Butler.

While the soldiers were billeted in barns, the officers were
assigned to a room in a French household. This usually was
the largest room on the ground floor, and all that is missing
from the picture is the huge four-poster bed. The only
available fuel was the armload of green saplings cut that
afternoon by the wood-cutting detail.   *December 1917.*

BILLETS

*I*T WAS a novel sensation to American troops to be billeted among the inhabitants of the many tiny farming villages. Barracks or camps would have formed an inviting target for enemy air-craft. Each house had its quota posted up beside the door, and, being house and barn in one, there was generally a room for one officer, forty men in the hay-loft, and eight horses in the stable.   *December 1917.*

MERRY CHRISTMAS 1917

ᵀHE "Lines of Communication" (which later became the
very efficient S. O. S.) failed about this time. The only shoes
to be had were size six. These were just the thing in Mexico,
but were about three sizes too small for cold, swollen feet.
Old torn uniforms, no gloves, just barely enough food, and
no forage, with the bitter cold and never ceasing manœuvres
on the bleak "WASHINGTON CENTRE," brought many a com-
parison with the winter at Valley Forge. And yet, the children were not forgotten. Each village had its Christmas tree
and party, organized and financed by the American soldiers.

"C'EST LA GUERRE!"

Many attachments, for the most part temporary, were made during the stay in the billeting area. The large size shoes had arrived and, to make matters worse, orders came to carry an extra pair in the pack. Campaign hats were replaced with trench caps and steel helmets, while both the French and the English gas masks were carried.   *January 1918.*

THE GYPSY BAND

O<small>LD</small> soldiers carry all their comforts with them. During the months spent in the training area they had gathered a few more articles than the regulations called for. The shortage of forage during the winter had reduced the horses almost to skeletons, so the march to the Toul Sector over sleet covered roads became a serious problem. *January 1918.*

THE TOUL SECTOR

*F*IFTEEN miles north of the city of Toul lay the famous five miles of front on which so many American divisions received their baptism of fire. Mont Sec, a sugar-loaf hill just inside the German lines, rose four hundred feet above the swampy Woevre Plain and gave the enemy perfect observation of all that went on for a depth of several miles. Here on the night of January 18th elements of the First Division entered the front lines. Dawn found them jointly holding the sector with the French First Moroccan Division under the eyes from Mont Sec.   *January 1918.*

FRENCH TYPES

GRADUALLY American units replaced French until the entire divisional sector was occupied. The First Moroccan Division had many types which were new to the Americans. Composed mainly of the Foreign Legion and colonial regiments from North Africa, it scarcely seemed a part of the usual French Army in horizon blue. Speaking Arabic and other strange languages, these veterans of many battles, in olive drab uniforms, formed one of the greatest fighting units.   *January 1918.*

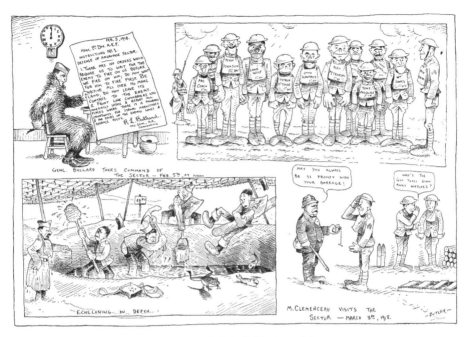

AN AMERICAN SECTOR AT LAST

ON FEBRUARY 5th, General Bullard, commanding the First Division, took over the command of the Toul Sector. General Pershing had selected the St. Mihiel Salient as the first American objective. Consequently the Lines of Communication, the Gondrecourt area and the Toul Sector on the south side of the salient were turned over to the Americans. This sector had been quiet since 1914, but its character was immediately changed by American command and preparations for future action. *February 1918.*

THE COMMUNICATION TRENCH

*F*ROM January until April, the First Division occupied the three-year-old trenches of the Toul Sector. Scarcely a day passed when it did not rain, sleet or snow. The engineers and the infantry worked incessantly on new positions to prepare the sector against attack, while carrying parties and reliefs ploughed up and down the communication trenches.

February 1918.

VISITING GENERALS

'T'HE stream of visitors, both French and American, seemed endless. A few were taken down into the infantry positions, but the majority, arriving by daylight, were shown the batteries of the 5th Field Artillery in the Forêt de la Reine. As it was impossible to dig deep in the mud, it was necessary to maintain casemated shelters, duck-board walks, and elaborate camouflage.   *February 1918.*

FRENCH TELEPHONES

𝒯HE combination of poorly insulated wires run close to the ground and French centrals made telephoning an art. Even the officers of the French Mission with the First Division had difficulties. *March 1918.*

THE EYES OF THE DIVISION

AT COMMANDING points in each sector were constructed splinter-proof shelters with blankets at all openings to protect against gas. Here trained observers watched every movement in enemy territory, located enemy batteries, and recorded all enemy activity. The appearance of a single German was instantly reported by telephone to a battery which promptly replied with a round of shrapnel. *March 1918.*

PAS DE GAZ

*T*HE Germans retaliated by firing on sensitive points at night just when the rations were being carried forward. So rigid had been the "gas discipline" that the arrival of a few duds, sounding to the inexperienced ear like gas shells, caused many a false alarm. In every position there was always a gas sentry whose duty it was to sound the alarm and send up a green rocket.   *March 1918.*

NIGHT BOMBING

DIVISION and Artillery Brigade Headquarters at Menil-la-Tour were frequently the target of German airplanes. Often there was as much danger from falling anti-aircraft shells as from the bombs themselves. The quick jump from a warm bed to a wet trench created a fine camaraderie between all ranks and arms of the service. *March 1918.*

"SIR, MY ORDERS ARE ——"

As soon as the infantry called for a protective barrage the sentry, always on duty with each gun, threw the fused shell lying on the trail into the gun and fired the first round. This brought the remainder of the gun crew to their posts and the firing continued. Each gun was laid on its part of the normal barrage, and other barrage positions were marked on the board. The Brigade Commander, on his incessant inspections, demanded a recitation by each sentry of the standing orders for his post.   *March 1918.*

AN ARTILLERY DUEL

*I*N SOME parts of the sector, the front line trenches were but fifty yards apart. As soon as General Bullard called for activity, there began a series of trench raids by both sides. These were miniature attacks preceded by artillery fire and sometimes were made by a raiding party of more than two hundred men. To protect the infantry against these attacks, the artillery stood ready to fire barrages. Often a nervous sentry would precipitate a first-class artillery duel by shooting up the colored flare which called for a barrage. Then the cannoneers did all the work, while the infantry had all the fun.

March 1918.

NEWS OF THE GERMAN SPRING OFFENSIVE

THE long expected German offensive came on the 21st of March and soon the enemy was sweeping down across Picardy towards the Channel Ports. Each day the communiqués showed further advances. Fighting in the open was an attractive prospect to the Infantry Major whose battalion headquarters was a dugout deep with mud.

March 1918.

OFF FOR THE BIG SHOW

℃HE First Division did not have long to wait. Relieved
from the Toul sector by the 26th Division between April
1st and 3rd, it sped westward across France in forty standard
troop trains.   *April 1918.*

"THE EYES OF THE WORLD ARE UPON YOU"

A week at Chaumont-en-Vexin was spent in brushing up on open warfare tactics. General Pershing, as well as the staff of the First French Army to which the First Division had been assigned, watched its training with great interest, for these were the first American troops to go into the great battle. At the close of the week, General Pershing called together the officers and, to the accompaniment of the rumble of heavy artillery, told them of their mission, of their responsibilities and of his confidence in them.   *April 1918.*

THE FOOT ARTILLERY

A FOUR-DAY march brought the Division to the billeting area behind the Montdidier front. The artillery horses had become so thin from exposure and lack of forage during the winter that the entire personnel of the Artillery Brigade was compelled to march on foot and carry their packs.

April 1918.

REFUGEES

As THE troops marched up to the front, they passed the refugees moving southward. Families, whose men between the ages of eighteen and forty-eight were in the army, took what they could hastily pack and quit their homes with the full knowledge that what they left was gone forever.

April 1918.

"DAMN THAT OBSERVATION BALLOON"

How different from the winter in Lorraine was the spring in Picardy. Untouched as yet by the war, the gentle rolling farm lands and quaint villages so recently deserted were a welcome sight to the tired troops. But even far behind the lines it was not safe to walk in daylight. German captive balloons adjusted artillery fire on everything that moved.

April 1918.

BATTERY POSITIONS IN PICARDY

*A*T FIRST there were no deeply dug or well sheltered battery positions on the Cantigny-Montdidier front. Batteries went into position on the side of the road or in the open fields, and trusted to camouflage nets to protect them from observation. Once a battery was located on the map by airplane photographs, the range was quickly adjusted by triangulation on air-bursts of shells fitted with time fuses. Then even the shallow trench under the camouflage net was welcome.

April 1918.

THE FRONT LINE IN PICARDY

𝒯HE front lines had stabilized in a wheatfield. By day the infantry lay in shallow fox-holes and during the short night, while the one meal of the day was brought up, they dug furiously in the hard chalky soil to connect these holes into a trench line. At no point was this protected by barbed wire, for every attempt to erect wire brought quick bursts of machine gun fire. These trenches were lightly held. At intervals along the front, a squad of eight men held a strong point, while sergeants and officers crawled from post to post.

April 1918.

GAS ATTACK AT M. N. D.

Telephone wires, no matter how carefully laid, caused ground currents which could occasionally be picked up by enemy "listening-in" posts. Accordingly, all units were known by code letters and their commanding officers and staffs by the names of months. "June" (signal officer) "M. N. D." (2nd Battalion 6th Field Artillery) had acquired miscellaneous pets left in a neighboring village by the French peasants in their flight. Gas was used constantly on these positions and the "gas discipline" was very efficient. *May 1918.*

ANOTHER PARTY AT VILLERS TOURNELLE

Two infantry regiments held the front lines, while the other two went into reserve. The system of defense consisted of a lightly held front line, behind this a stronger second line, and a "line of resistance" where the supporting troops were concentrated. The only available shelter in this third line was the villages of Broyes and Villers Tournelle, where were established the two regimental headquarters. The Germans, quick to sense this, concentrated on these villages the bulk of their shell fire. One night, fifteen thousand rounds of high explosive and mustard gas fell on Villers Tournelle in less than three and one-half hours.   *May 1918*.

THE FIRST AMERICAN ATTACK—CANTIGNY

AMERICAN troops had been in France eleven months. Aside from holding a few quiet sectors, they had done nothing and there was some doubt among the Allies as to their value as combat troops. Upon the insistent demands of the Americans for a test, the French High Command permitted an attack on the village of Cantigny, the commanding point of the sector. Observers of the Allied Armies were on hand to watch the assault. The complete success proved that two million combat troops had been added to the Allies.

May 1918.

MOPPING UP

AT DAWN on May 28th, after an hour's artillery preparation, the 28th Infantry, assisted by French tanks and a
detachment of French flame throwers, assaulted and captured the village. There was hand to hand fighting in and
among the shattered buildings, but the final objective was
reached on schedule time and two hundred and thirty prisoners were captured. Holding the village against seven counter-attacks during the next three days was a far greater task
than its capture.   *May 1918.*

THE HORSE LINES

*H*IDDEN from airplane observation, the artillerymen not
serving the guns lived back in the Bois de Tartigny. They
spent the day grooming and watering horses and standing
inspection. As night fell, the emaciated animals were led out
to open fields to graze. A soldier holding the halter ropes of
four horses got little rest, especially on clear nights when
enemy airplanes dropped bombs.   *May 1918.*

THE LOST AVIATOR

During the assault on Cantigny, a contact plane dropped messages to Division Headquarters which showed the position of the advancing lines. A soldier was detailed to retrieve these messages from where they dropped in the field. Later, a confused Allied aviator, believing he was over the enemy lines, flew low over the sector. The plane had Allied markings. The same soldier was present. Something dropped from the plane. The soldier ran eagerly to get the message and then— ! * ! * ! * ! *   *June 1918.*

SNIPING WITH THE HEAVIES

A HIGH-POWERED telescope, good visibility and the refine-
ments of modern gunnery made sniping with a six-inch
howitzer at a range of several miles one of the enlivening
features of this sector. Seldom has big game shooting been so
highly organized or so effective. *June 1918.*

THE DAYLIGHT RAID

A sergeant of regimental headquarters, 18th Infantry, believing in the success of the unexpected, led a small patrol through the wheat in broad daylight to a known enemy post. The sentry, confident that movement by day-light in this sector was impossible, was caught unawares, tapped on the head and dragged back. Half way, they remembered his machine gun, returned for it, and left a receipt for both.

June 1918.

METHODICAL SHELLING

It DID not take the Germans long to locate important head-quarters. In retaliation for the capture of Cantigny, they brought up some big howitzers. Fortunately, the methodical Teuton mind caused them to be fired at regular ten minute intervals, so that the cellar of the big chateau afforded an effective refuge.   *June 1918.*

THE SONG OF THE G. I. CAN

OUT in the open the shells from the siege howitzers, because of their high trajectory and low velocity, could be heard coming for many seconds. From a distant whine the sound grew to a roaring growl which rose to a terrifying screech as the shell "came in." The soldiers, likening these shells to the huge Galvnized Iron barrels used for cooking and sundry other purposes, called them "G. I. Cans."   *June 1918.*

BRINGING HOME THE BACON

IT SOON became evident to the French High Command that the Germans were preparing to resume the offensive in this vicinity. Information of the enemy's intentions was essential and could best be obtained from prisoners. Regularly, raiding parties went out from the four regiments and in spite of all the enemy could do, scarcely a night passed that a terrified prisoner was not in the division cage before dawn.

June 1918.

ONE IN THE GUN—THREE IN THE AIR

𝒯HE information from prisoners was correct. On June 6th the First Division took up new defensive positions and on June 9th, the Germans attacked along the entire front from Montdidier to Noyon. During four long days and nights the firing never ceased, over thirty thousand rounds a day being fired on the division front. Regardless of enemy counter battery fire, the guns were served so faithfully that the enemy's attack failed to reach the support line.   *June 1918.*

A HORSE SHOW AT THE FRONT

WHEN the First Division began its march to the Picardy front in April there were doubts that the artillery horses, exhausted by the rigors of the winter and weak from lack of forage, could pull the guns and caissons. Drastic action saved the situation. The Artillery Brigade was dismounted and every spare moment of day or night was spent in grazing and grooming. So rapid was the recovery, that a horse show was held in the woods behind Division Headquarters on July 4th. The winning teams received cash prizes and three-day passes to Paris. *July 1918.*

THE WINNING EMPLACEMENT

꒯HE 4th of July competition extended also to battery positions. Their gun crews, constantly under enemy fire and constantly firing in support of their infantry, had developed a pride not only in firing technique, but also in the smartness of their emplacements. Flowers, curtains, rugs and other domestic comforts brought from neighboring abandoned villages adorned the gun pits. *July 1918.*

FIRST MUSTARD GAS SHELLS

*F*OR months the Americans had suffered from repeated con-
centrations of German mustard gas without the chance to
retaliate in kind. It was known that the French had on hand a
limited supply of these shells, but were holding them in
reserve for emergencies. Captain Butler drew for the
"Observer" this cartoon of the fancied arrival of a load of
mustard gas shells in a battery position. This drawing was
judiciously circulated among the French High Command
and, as a result, 6,000 rounds arrived for the First Division
and were fired as a national salute on the 4th of July.

July 1918.

RELIEVED

AFTER 78 days in the Montdidier sector, the ease of a rest
billet with its strange quiet, absence of gas mask and helmet,
and the reappearance of three square meals a day, gave the
opportunity for mind and body to relax.   *July 1918.*

THE PARIS TRAIN

WHILE the Division was moving from Picardy, a few
found it necessary to go to Paris on "official business."
July 1918.

THE BATTLE OF PARIS

A BATTALION from each of the Allied Armies came to
Paris and marched in the memorable parade of July 14th,
1918, with the enemy but forty miles away. That night the
military police stopped every soldier and read to him the
order recalling all leaves.   *July 1918.*

JOINING MANGIN'S TENTH ARMY

At the end of a long march from Picardy to the north of Paris the Division, anticipating a period of rest and replacement, found long lines of French trucks waiting to transport its troops and field guns. While the horse-drawn elements moved by forced marches, the balance of the Division rode for twenty hours, forty men to a truck, to the edge of the forest of Villers Cotterets. At dusk began the memorable march to the front. Tanks, guns, reel-carts, staff cars, machine guns, armored cars, and slat wagons overcrowded the roads. The infantry moved up as best they could. *July 1918.*

THE SURPRISE ATTACK

WITHOUT the slightest warning, Mangin's Army, with the First American Division, the First Moroccan Division and the Second American Division forming the spearhead, leapt forward at dawn on the 18th of July at the one vital spot in the German lines. Taken by complete surprise, whole battalions of the enemy were captured in support line dugouts. *July 1918.*

"RIDE 'EM—COWBOY"

So RAPID was the progress of the first day's advance that in a few hours the guns went forward at a gallop to the Paris-Soissons Road. *July 1918.*

THROUGH THE WHEAT

𝒯HE timely arrival of German motorised machine-gun battalions enabled the enemy to consolidate a formidable line of
resistance beyond the Paris-Soissons road. The infantry
fought their way forward without assistance from the tanks,
which, by then, had all been knocked out by direct hits from
enemy field guns.   *July 1918.*

SOISSONS

LIEUTENANT: "Hey! What's the idea of shooting at those Moroccans?"

SOLDIER: "Moroccans? Hell, I thought them was Turks and I knowed the Turks was fighting with the Boches!"

July 1918.

THE FRENCH CAVALRY CHARGE

LATE in the afternoon of the first day two regiments of
French Cavalry attacked, but machine guns, wire and enemy
planes were too great an obstacle.   *July 1918.*

DIVISION HEADQUARTERS

A HUGE underground quarry in the hillside overlooking the village of Cœuvres made an excellent headquarters. The more important of the various members of the division staff had large blocks of stone for tables. Cooking was done in one corner, surgery in another, prisoners were questioned in a third, while staff officers from the corps argued in all directions. Meanwhile, the routine of directing an advancing division was maintained. *July 1918.*

BRIGADE HEADQUARTERS

𝒯HE First Infantry Brigade occupied a trench near Chaudun.
A brigade headquarters consisted of a general of infantry, a
colonel of artillery, and someone to work the telephone.

July 1918.

A PRISONER OF WAR

*E*ACH nationality looked upon the prisoners with a different point of view. The attitudes of the New Zealander on
the armored car, the lancer, the Scotchman, the wounded
Frenchman, the doughboy, and the Moroccan varied.

July 1918.

RELIEVED BY THE SCOTCH

Aᴄᴛᴇʀ five days of constant fighting, the welcome sound of bagpipes heralded the relief of the sector by the Fifteenth Scottish Division. Before dawn on the 23rd the American infantry was out of action, but the artillery stayed over two days to help the Scotch attack.   *July 1918.*

A QUIET SECTOR

AFTER the relief at Soissons, the Division was moved by
rail back to Lorraine and took over the Saizerais sector near
Pont-à-Mousson. This was one of the quietest sectors on the
front and both sides were content to let it so remain.

August 1918.

BIARRITZ

MEANWHILE, a few of the more fortunate obtained a few days' leave at the watering places on the French coast.

August 1918.

VAUCOULEURS

*R*ELIEVED from the Saizerais sector, the Division soon
realized that another attack was in preparation. Staff officers
with maps, manœuvres of all arms and meticulous attention
to details of material and equipment, left little doubt that
the next operation would take place in the Toul sector and
that the dreaded Mont Sec was to be captured at last.

September 1918.

MOVING UP FOR ST. MIHIEL

ONCE more the First Division re-occupied the Toul sector, this time as part of the army attacking the St. Mihiel salient. Far different from the hasty preparations for the Soissons attack, months had been spent in plans for this action, the first of the war to be undertaken independently by an American Army.   *September 1918.*

DOUGHBOYS

*I*N ADDITION to the standard full field equipment which is supposed to be the maximum weight a soldier should carry, the infantry of the First Division carried a few more supplies, among others: wire-cutters, a sack of hand grenades, a sack of rifle grenades, two extra bandoliers of rifle ammunition, a prismatic compass, a reel of telephone wire, an additional canteen and an armload of clips for the Chauchat automatic rifle.   *September 1918.*

ST. MIHIEL

*F*OLLOWING a rolling barrage through the old no-man's-land
of the Toul sector, over acres of rusty barbed wire and on
past Mont Sec, went the First Division as the left flank of
the two Corps attacking from the South.   *September 1918.*

ON THE FINAL OBJECTIVE

SHORTLY after dawn on the second day of the attack, the First Division met the Twenty-Sixth Division in Vigneulles, at the foot of the range of hills. The Germans had retreated, burning everything they could not carry. The St. Mihiel salient was captured with unexpected ease and the Division had the new experience of "digging in" with no enemy in sight. *September 13, 1918.*

THE ANSWER TO THE MACHINE GUN

*I*N THE St. Mihiel attack "baby tanks" manned by Americans demonstrated their value.　　　*September 1918.*

SOUVENIRS

In THEIR hasty flight, the Germans left much behind which
the Americans collected. To restore mobility to the Division, orders were issued stripping it of all "salvage."

September 1918.

MOVING INTO THE MEUSE-ARGONNE

GREATER preparations were necessary for this attack. In addition to the usual traffic, material had to be brought up to restore the roads so that supplies could follow as the troops advanced; consequently, the roads were soon congested far beyond their capacity. *September 1918.*

A QUIET DAY IN RESERVE NEAR THE TOWN OF VERY UNTIL——

𝒯HE rolling country between the high wooded plateau of
the Argonne Forest and the Meuse River afforded excellent
cover in which even an observation balloon was quite safe.
October 1918.

————A DARING ENEMY AVIATOR SETS FIRE TO OUR SAUSAGE

Diving from a tremendous height with motor shut off, an enemy airplane ignited the balloon with incendiary bullets and was away before the anti-aircraft guns could fire effectively. The other arms went into action more quickly. Everybody did his bit on these occasions.   *October 1918.*

DUG-IN

AFTER every advance the infantry immediately dug in
under machine gun and rifle fire from the wooded crests,
which seemed always to surround the troops. To reply was
almost impossible, for the gun muzzles were hidden and the
firing came from everywhere.   *October 1918.*

ADVANCING

*W*HEN the advance was resumed, nests of machine guns in the clumps of woods were cleaned out one by one. Hill 240, with its flanking fire, was a constant menace until captured.

October 1918.

AMMUNITION, RATIONS, AND REPLACEMENTS

AMERICAN water tanks, French wine vats, Ford ambu-
lances, every kind of horse and motor drawn vehicle including America's contribution, the prairie schooner, filled the
roads.   *October 1918.*

THE EXERMONT RAVINE

Prisoners were not as plentiful as at Soissons. Each lot marching to the rear marked another woods captured by bitter hand-to-hand fighting, for the German High Command had ordered the line just north of the ravine to be held at all costs. *October 1918.*

ONLY A BIRD IN A GILDED CAGE

Colonels of German infantry were not often caught, but
the First Division bagged one in the Meuse-Argonne.
October 1918.

THE GERMAN MACHINE GUN

*H*ATED and feared more than any other weapon in the war
was the German heavy machine gun. No one ever doubted
the bravery of the gun crews, few of which were ever taken
prisoner. As the advancing waves rolled over them, the
guns were fired until the last. *October 1918.*

PREPARING FOR ATTACK OF NOVEMBER FIRST

STAFF OFFICER: Shouldn't those guns be pushed back in
the woods a little farther?

LIEUTENANT: Sir, if we were to shove them back it would
push the guns at the back of the wood out in the open.

October 1918.

THE LIBERATED VILLAGES

*B*Y THE first week in November, the advance between the Meuse and the Argonne gained momentum and villages were reached whose inhabitants had been under forced German rule since 1914.   *November 1918.*

THE MARCH ON SEDAN

SUDDENLY the German line gave way and the Allies rushed in. Ahead lay the historic city of Sedan. Eager to capture a large city, the Americans sent the First Division on this mission. In thirty hours it marched and fought its way forward thirty-eight miles through the German rear guards. On the outskirts of Sedan the Division halted on orders from Allied Headquarters to permit the French division, whose home was Sedan, to enter first. *November 1918*.

THE ARMISTICE—FRONT AND REAR

To the troops in the line, the Armistice came as simply
another halt in the day's march, and everyone wondered how
long it would last. In Paris everyone knew it would last
forever.   *November 11th, 1918.*

THE ARMY OF OCCUPATION

T<small>HE</small> Armistice did not bring an end to military duties. The long, hard march up to the Rhine was led by the oldest and most experienced divisions. The First Division had the honor of being the first to cross, and took its place on the thirty-mile bridgehead beyond Coblenz. Here it remained until August and was the last of the fighting divisions to return home. *1918–1919*.

"DIE WACHT AM RHEIN"

WITH the Stars and Stripes flying from the castle of Ehrenbreitstein, the Army of Occupation was made a model of military efficiency. The ardor of American military police made leave areas in southern France a necessity.

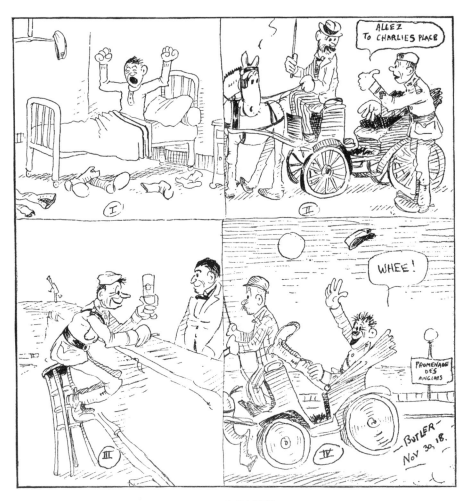

A DAY AT NICE

[Photographed from Guest Book at Charlie's Bar]

PARIS DURING THE PEACE CONFERENCE

Eᴀᴄʜ of the Allied Nations established an impressive headquarters in Paris so as to collect their share of the spoils. Odd
and exotic uniforms filled the streets, theatres, cafes, and taxi
cabs. The occasional combat soldier, on leave from the
Army of Occupation, found the competition brisk.

FACES AND FIGURES FAMILIAR . . . .

‴HE First Division, as the first to withstand enemy attacks
and the first to advance into enemy territory, was constantly
called upon to supply experienced leaders for its own and
other combat units.

. . . . TO THE FIRST DIVISION A. E. F.

AFTER each major engagement many officers were promoted to higher commands. Some went to other divisions and army corps where their experience was of great value in training and in battle.

HOME

It's home, boys, home, that's where we want to be
Home once more in the land of liberty
And we'll nail Old Glory to the top of the pole
And we'll all re-enlist in a pig's necktie.

Early in September 1919, the First Division, as the escort of General Pershing, debarked in New York and paraded with full equipment down Fifth Avenue and later in Washington. The First Division, which had been given the honor of leading the American Army to France, had earned the honor of being the last to return. This marked the termination of the American Expeditionary Forces.

September 1919.

THE ORDERLY ROOM AT VALHALLA

*B*UCK privates from all former wars greet the latest arrival,
the veteran of the FIRST DIVISION.

"The Commander-in-Chief has noted in this division a special pride of service and a high state of morale never broken by hardship nor battle."

*General Order No. 201,
Headquarters American Expeditionary Forces
1918*

AFTERWORD

BY the time Alban Butler, Jr. published *"Happy Days!"* in 1928, the surviving veterans of the First Division were well into their postwar lives and probably not especially conscious of the special group of men they had been or of the legacy they had created. Yet both were remarkable.

First Division veterans played important roles in the interwar Army as well as in civilian life. Butler himself became a successful oilman. The man for whom he served as aide throughout World War I, General Charles P. Summerall, commanded the division through Soissons, St. Mihiel, and much of the Meuse-Argonne, remained in the Army, and rose to be its chief of staff in 1929. After retirement, he was president of the Citadel for many years. In addition, Colonel Teddy Roosevelt, Jr., commander of the 26th Infantry Regiment, resigned from the Army, helped found the American Legion, held important posts in the Harding and Hoover administrations, and enjoyed a successful business career. He returned to military duty in World War II and served valiantly as a brigadier general with the 1st and 4th Infantry Divisions until his death from a heart attack in France in July 1944.

FACES AND FIGURES FAMILIAR TO THE FIRST DIVISION AEF
Brigadier General Frank Parker, Lieutenant Colonel Theodore Roosevelt, Jr., and Mrs. Eleanor Butler Roosevelt, at Romagne, Meuse, France, on November 13, 1918. Roosevelt, the son of President Teddy Roosevelt, would serve as the First Division's assistant commanding general during World War II.

Colonel Clarence G. Huebner, a captain at the Battle of Cantigny in May 1918, became a general officer and commanded his old division in perhaps its most difficult and most important fight at Omaha Beach in Normandy, France, on June 6, 1944. At Cantigny with Huebner was Major Robert R. McCormick, commanding the 1st Battalion, 5th Field

Artillery. Promoted to colonel during the war, he used that title thereafter as owner of the Chicago Tribune Company and publisher of the *Chicago Tribune*.

Also on the battlefield at Cantigny was Private Samuel Ervin, who shed his doughboy uniform to pursue a career in politics, leading to the United States Senate and chairmanship of the Watergate Commission. Undoubtedly, Ervin knew a fellow North Carolinian, Lieutenant Samuel I. "Si" Parker. Parker's heroism at Soissons was recognized after the war with the Medal of Honor, by which time he was active in his community, serving on several boards and foundations. His wounds had rendered him unfit for field duty in World War II, but he resumed active duty as a lieutenant colonel and taught leadership at the Infantry Officer Candidate School at Fort Benning, Georgia.

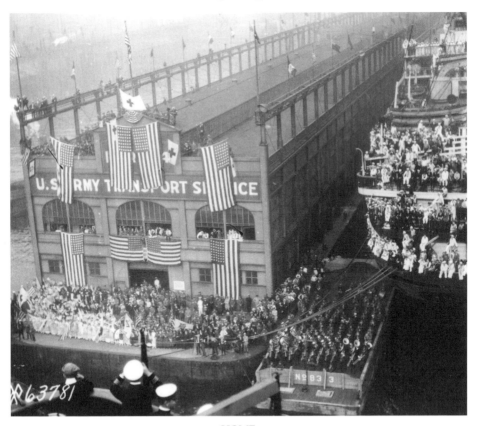

HOME
General Pershing arrived with the First Division on the USS *Leviathan* at New York, September 8, 1919. This was the former German passenger liner *Vaterland*, seized by the United States in 1917 and used as a troopship. This picture was donated by William Steamer, General Summerall's chauffer.

Of the many, many more, perhaps no person had as much an impact on American history as the young officer who, as First Division operations officer, planned the attack on Cantigny: George C. Marshall. Marshall was to become chief of staff of the U.S. Army during World War II, an architect of victory in that conflict, a confidant to Presidents Franklin Roosevelt and Harry Truman, secretary of defense, and, later, secretary of state, and the man for whom the post-World War II Marshall Plan was named.

These remarkable men served in a remarkable outfit that had a remarkable future. The First Division was one of only four divisions the Army retained through the lean interwar years. With its headquarters eventually established at Governors Island in New York Harbor and its regiments scattered up and down

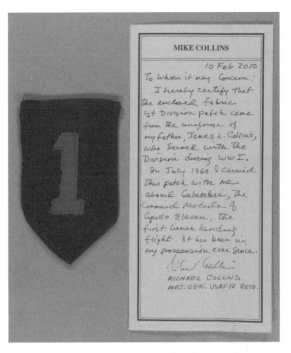

THE BIG RED ONE

This World War I First Division patch was carried by astronaut Michael Collins, pilot of the Apollo 11 Lunar Command Module *Columbia*, as he orbited the moon during the first moon walk with Neil Armstrong and Buzz Aldrin. Collins carried this "Big Red One" patch with him as part of the allotted personal items that each astronaut was allowed on the mission. It belonged to his father, James L. Collins, who ultimately retired as a Major General. During World War I, James Collins led a battalion of the 7th Field Artillery, First Division in France. Before the AEF operations in France, his father was General Pershing's aide during the pursuit of Pancho Villa to the Durango Line.

the East Coast, the division managed to preserve a cohesive identity and *esprit* on which to build once mobilization occurred in 1940. Reorganized in 1939 as the 1st Infantry Division (to distinguish it from the new armor divisions and, later, airborne divisions), the division assembled first at Camp Devens, Massachusetts. Wearing the distinctive red numeral "1" the doughboys fashioned at the end of World War I, the 1st Infantry Division was the first deployed to Europe, in August 1942. It stormed ashore in North Africa in November 1942 and fought across Algeria and Tunisia. It was first ashore in Sicily in July 1943 and again on Omaha Beach in June 1944. Hard fighting across Europe followed, including a heroic stand on the north shoulder of the Battle of the Bulge that helped turn that battle for the Allies. By Victory in Europe Day on May 8, 1945, the "Big Red One," as the division now called itself, was becoming legendary. Aided by the Society of the First Division, which the doughboys founded in 1919, the 1st Infantry Division's "special pride in service" would not be broken by the hardships or the battles of Vietnam and Desert Storm or in the Balkans, Iraq, or Afghanistan.

Perhaps no better evidence of the powerful *esprit* of the First Division captured in *"Happy Days!"* is this: when astronaut Michael Collins was allowed to take a few small personal tokens with him to the moon in 1969 on Apollo 11, among them was one of his father's prized possessions: his Big Red One shoulder patch from his "happy" days as a doughboy of the First Division.

—Paul Herbert
Executive Director
First Division Museum at Cantigny,
Robert R. McCormick Foundation
Wheaton, Illinois
Winter 2011